THE DAY ANNABELLE WAS BITTEN BY A DOODLEBUG

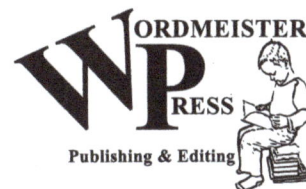

2017 WRITER'S DIGEST
HONORABLE MENTION
SELF-PUBLISHED BOOK AWARDS

Wordmeister Press
Publishing & Editing

For Annabelle.
Thank you for inspiring me!

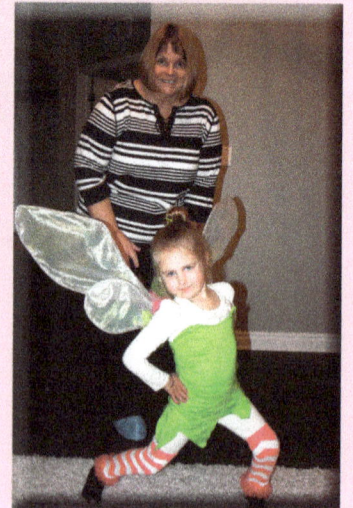

Love, Grammie

When Annabelle woke, the day was quite sunny
But Annabelle said, "I feel kind of funny."
Her fingers were itchy. She felt a bit dizzy.
"I MUST doodle NOW!" she shrieked in a tizzy.

She jumped on the bed. She was going berserk!
"Hey Mommy, please HURRY! I must get to work!"

She cried out for paper. She called for a pen.
Then started to doodle.... again and again.

She doodled some circles.

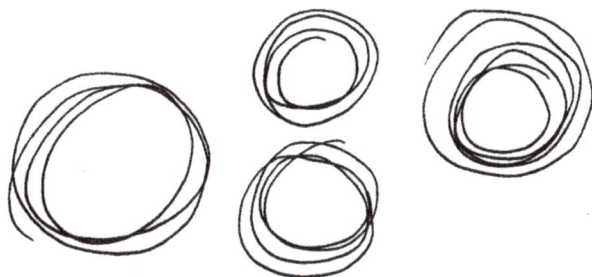

She doodled some squares.

She doodled some squiggles.

She doodled three bears.

She doodled a rainbow.

She doodled a girl.

a spiral,

She doodled a zigzag,

a swirl.

She doodled some flowers.

She doodled a star.

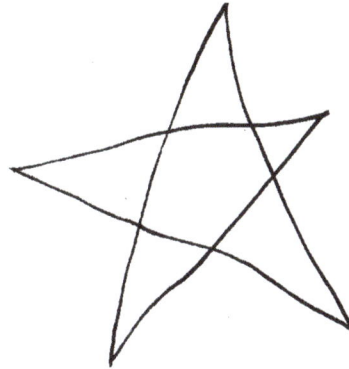

She doodled a poodle,

a bird,

and a car.

She doodled all day, from the morn till the night.
She doodled, determined, with no end in sight.

She doodled with markers. She doodled with pens.
She doodled with pencils, with chalk, and with crayons.

Dinnertime came. It was tuna and noodles.
But Annabelle couldn't stop drawing those doodles.

"I can't pause to eat now, " Belle wrinkled her brow.
"I should take a break, but I just don't know how!"

Her parents were worried. "Now get in the car.
We'll go see the doctor, it isn't too far."

With tablet in hand, she climbed into the seat
And doodled twelve drawings that looked really neat.

The doctor looked puzzled. He then checked her neck.
"A doodlebug bit her! See this tiny speck?"

Right there on her neck, smack dab in the middle -
A tiny red mark, a cute little scribble!
"But what should we do?" said her parents, aghast.
The doctor assured them, "This frenzy won't last."

His prescription? More paper!
They bought a huge stack
For oodles of doodles....
they couldn't keep track!

Belle doodled some hearts, then she doodled some cats
And three-headed creatures who wore goofy hats.

She doodled in bedrooms. She doodled in halls.
Her mommy cried, "Annabelle! Not on the walls!"
Since practice makes perfect, Belle stayed in the groove.
With every new doodle her talent improved.

Yes, Annabelle's life was now filled with her doodles.
Oodles and oodles and oodles of doodles.

She made artsy fabrics. She opened a shop.
Her wallpaper patterns were selling non-stop.

The newspaper came. Put her on the front page.

BREAKING NEWS!

Annabelle the amazing DOODLER

Her now-famous doodles became all the rage.

She traveled the world and she doodled on planes.

She doodled in limos, in boats, and on trains.

She visited England and spoke with the queen
"Your fleur-de-lis doodles?—the GREATEST I've seen!"
The prince himself praised her. "May I call you Belle?
You're truly an artist! You doodle so well!

"Your doodles belong in a famous museum
Where thousands—no millions—of people can see 'em"

Her art was displayed at a Paris exhibit
Where critics proclaimed it was "truly exquisite."

Her parents watched proudly but had to admit
They secretly wished that the bug hadn't bit!

Then one day Belle's urge simply vanished away.
She said to her Mommy, "Let's go out to play!"

The bite on her neck had now faded at last.
She put down her markers. Her cravings had passed.
Her daddy was joyful. Her mom filled with glee
"Our Annabelle's back now! She's happy and free!"

She closed up her shop and sold every last doodle.

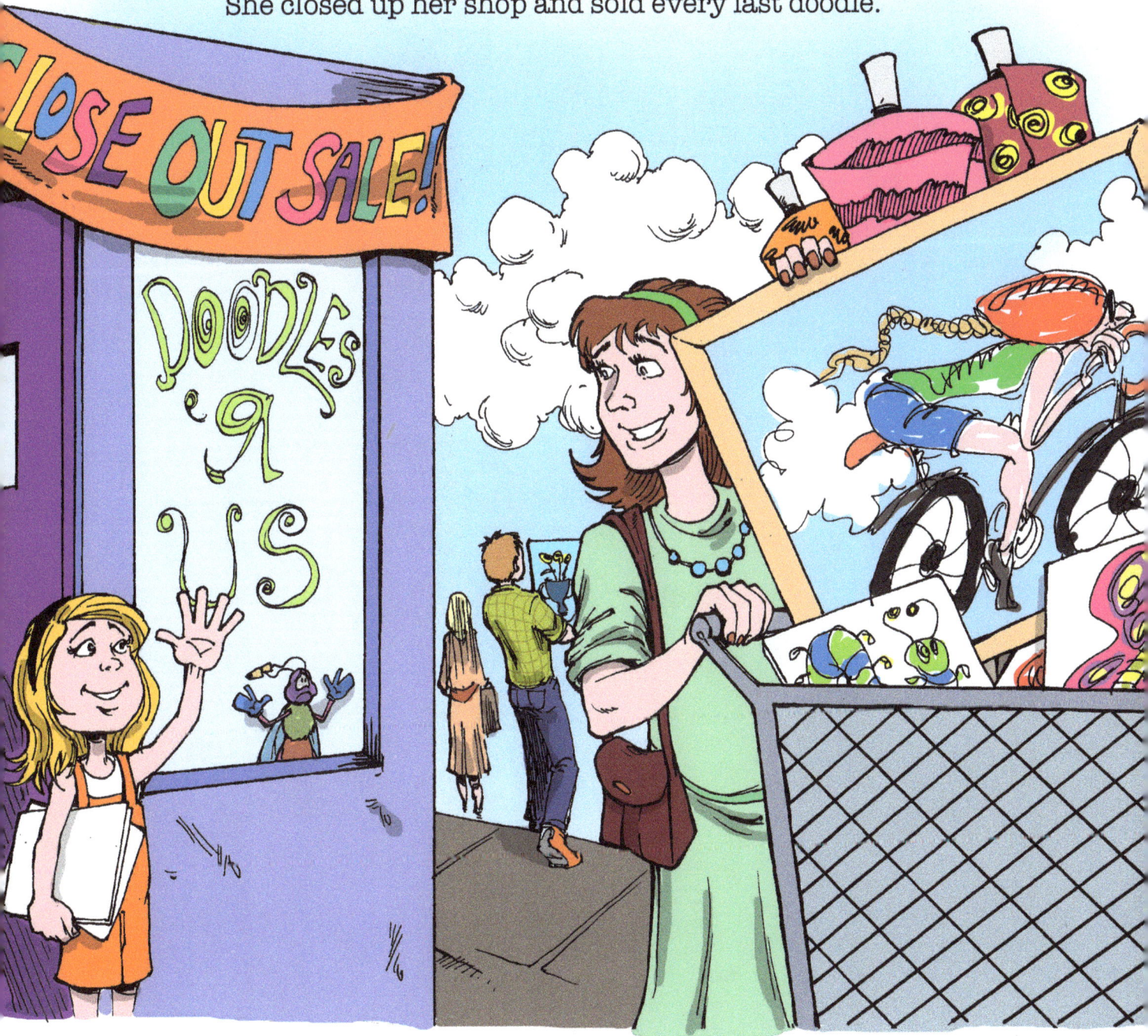

CLOSE OUT SALE!

DOODLES 'Я US

One customer purchased the kit and caboodle.

She went back to preschool, no longer so crazy.
She now loved to play with her sweet sister Maisie.

She once again jumped on her big trampoline
And kicked goals in soccer—the star of her team!

Though doodling ended, her art was still there
On every wrapped package, each couch and each chair.

She still likes to doodle, just on rare occasion
But Annabelle now needs a bit of persuasion.

The doodlebug? Well, he is hiding somewhere.
Is he in Belle's closet? Is he in Belle's hair?
Or is the bug waiting for one day when Maisie
Can pick up a crayon and draw a quick daisy?

When Belle's parents speak of those doodling days...
Then Annabelle laughs, "It was only a phase."
"It was kind of fun," she recalls with a shrug.
"To think it all happened because of a bug!"

Other books by Julie Wenzlick

Visit juliewenzlick.com

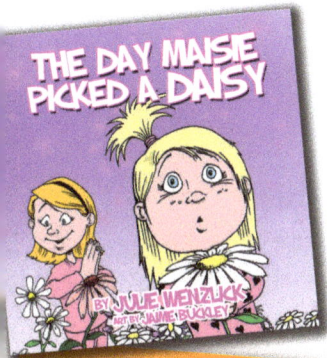

Big sister Annabelle decides to go against Mom's rules and take little sister Maisie Grace for a ride in her pink Barbie Corvette to see Miss Millie's garden. Join these wandering sisters as Maisie encounters a sign that she cannot read: Do NOT pick the Daisies! When she picks a daisy, these sisters are in for the adventure of lifetime! *Illustrated by Jaime Buckley.*

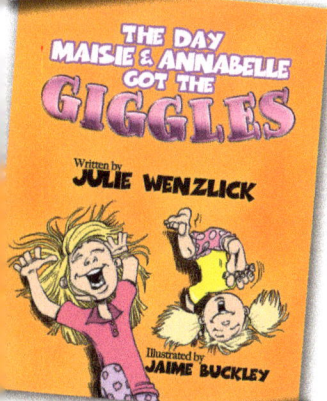

While jumping on the neighbor's trampoline, Annabelle and Maisie meet the colorful Gigglepuss. They suddenly burst into uncontrollable giggles. As they clutch their ribs and turn blue in the face from laughing so hard, Mommy and Daddy have no choice but to take them to the doctor. His unpleasant but very effective remedy finally brings them back to normal, but where is that rascally Gigglepuss, and who will be his next victim? *Illustrated by Jaime Buckley.*

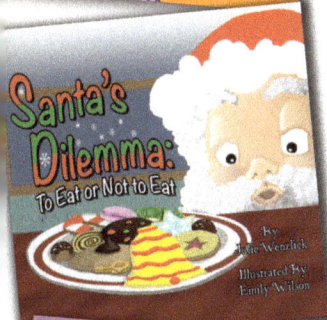

Oh Oh, Santa's in trouble! He has put on a few pounds and his Santa suit barely fits!   And now Mrs, Claus has come to the "rescue" with a new diet plan for Santa, STARTING on Christmas Eve! Follow Santa as he faces the Cookie Challenge at every house along his route. Will he stay on track for an entire night of cookie temptation? *Illustrated by Emily Wilson.*

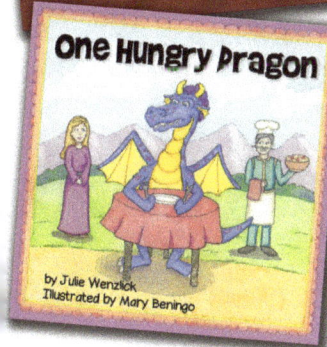

What's a dragon to do when everything he eats tastes like burnt toast? Ever since he was old enough to become a fire-breathing dragon, this dragon is starving! Knowing how dragons are "supposed" to behave, he demands a maiden to eat, causing some of the villagers to fear him. But deep down, the dragon only wants to find some way to eat food without having it burn. Can a clever princess find a way to help him? *Illustrated by Mary Beningo.*

About The Author

Julie Wenzlick is a retired English teacher and grandmother who loves to rhyme. **The Day Annabelle a was Bitten by a Doodlebug** is the first book of her series based on her granddaughters Annabelle and Maisie. This book earned one of the two Honorable Mentions from Writer's Digest in the Children's Picture Book category in the 25th annual Self-Published Book Awards.

She lives in Michigan with her husband Dan. Julie visits elementary classrooms to share her books and songs, hoping to inspire young children to start writing now! Find out more about Julie and all of her books at www.juliewenzlick.com.

About The Illustrator

Jaime Buckley is a popular parenting blogger, fiction author, illustrator and father of 12.

Best known for his **Wanted Hero** brand, he's the author of 29 books, a comic book series and created several games all based on his fantasy world. Jaime's GOSmiley™ game has continued to be a top-selling family game sold through Amazon and other outlets.

He lives in Utah with his wife Kathilynn, their nine children still at home and ten grandchildren close by.

You can learn more about Jaime by visiting either of his sites: JaimeBuckley.com or WantedHero.com.

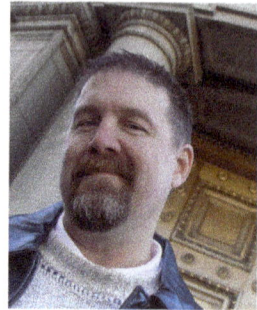

www.ingramcontent.com/pod-product-compliance
Lightning Source LLC
Chambersburg PA
CBHW040252100426
42811CB00011B/1238